PEGASUS ENCYCLOPEDIA LIBRARY

Physics
ELECTRICITY

Edited by: Anil Kumar Tomar, Pallabi B. Tomar
Managing editor: Tapasi De
Designed by: Vijesh Chahal, Anil Kumar and Rohit Kumar
Illustrated by: Suman S. Roy, Tanoy Choudhury
Colouring done by: Vinay Kumar, Sonu, Kiran Kumari & Pradeep Kumar

CONTENTS

What is electricity? 3
History of electricity 5
Basic properties of electric charges 6
Conductors and insulators 7
Methods of charging 9
Force between electric charges 11
Electric field 12
Electric flux 14
Electric potential 15
Capacitors and Capacitance 16
Combinations of Capacitors 17
Electric current 18
Ohm's Law 19
Resistance 20
Resistors in series 22
Resistors in Parallel 23
Electric Power 24
Magnetism 25
Magnetic field lines 26
Voltmeter 27
Ammeter 28
Wattmeter 29
Tips to save electricity 30
Test Your Memory 31
Index 32

What is electricity?

Electricity is one of the most important elements of our lives. It lights up our homes, cooks our food, powers our computers, televisions and most of the other devices. Electricity from batteries keeps our bikes and cars running, lets our laptops and mobiles work and makes our flashlights shine in the dark. To understand, what electricity is actually is, we should understand charge and charged particles.

There are two basic types of electric charges— positive charge and negative charge. If the same amounts of negative and positive charge are brought together in a system, they neutralize each other and there is no net charge of the system. The objects which contain positive and negative charges in equal amount are referred as neutral objects. If an object has more amount of one of the charge that is, positive or negative, then it is said to be electrically charged object.

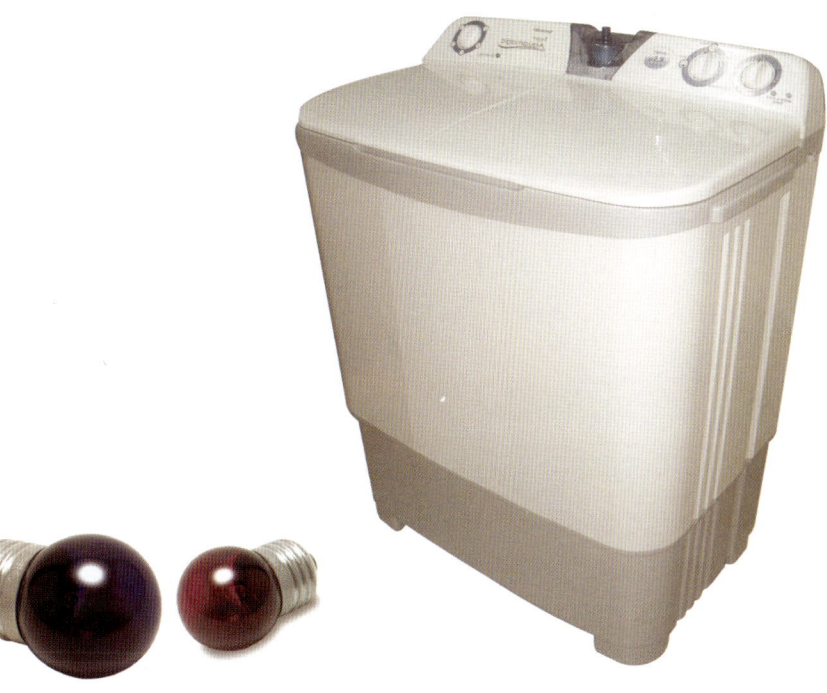

ELECTRICITY

We know that all matter is made up of atoms. The atoms, in turn, are made up of three subatomic particles - the proton, the neutron and the electron. The electrons and protons possess the equal amount of charge. A proton has positive charge while an electron has negative charge. The number of electrons surrounding the nucleus determines whether an atom is electrically charged or electrically neutral. The electrically neutral atoms contain equal numbers of protons and electrons while electrically charged atoms have unequal number of protons and electrons. The positively charged particles contain less number of electrons than protons while negatively charged particles contain more electrons than protons.

The unit of charge possessed by an object is coulomb. It is represented by symbol 'C'. One Coulomb of charge is very large quantity of charge. Thus, microCoulombs (μC) or nanoCoulombs (nC) are commonly used as the units of charge.

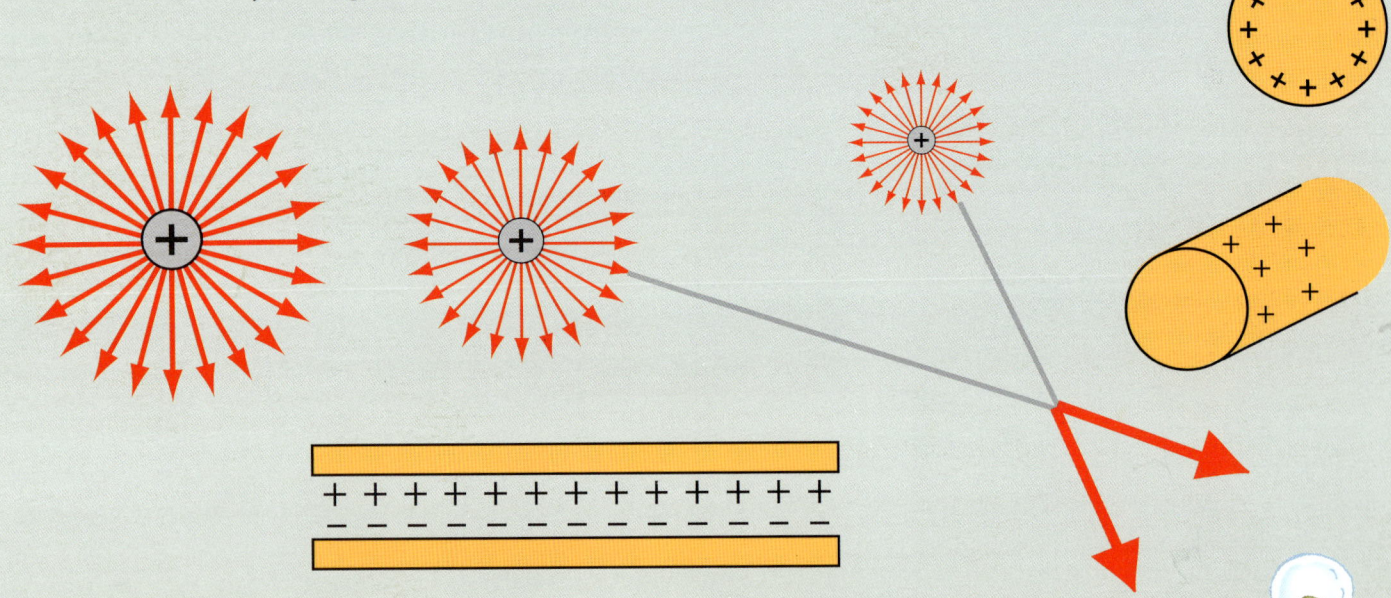

Do it yourself

Magnetize a balloon: Inflate an ordinary balloon. Then rub it briskly on a piece of fur, silk, nylon or wool. Now put the balloon against a wall and let go. Watch it 'stick' to the wall.

Explanation: By rubbing the balloon, you are covering it with lots of little negative charges. The negative charges are attracted to positive charges in the wall. In fact, they are so attracted they will hold the balloon against the wall.

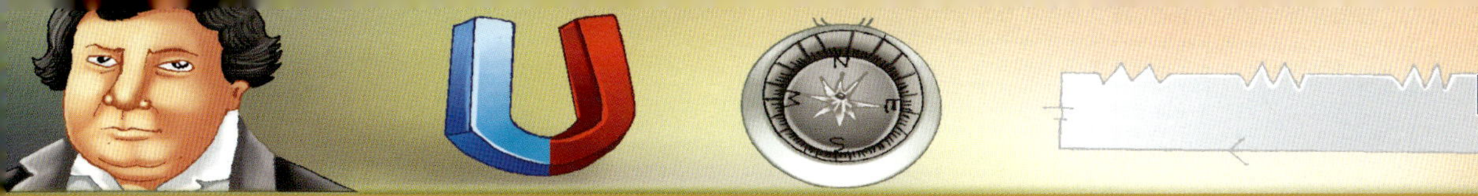

History of electricity

The electricity has always been around because it naturally exists in the world. Lightning is simply a flow of electrons between the ground and the clouds. When we touch something and get a shock, it is caused by static electricity moving towards us. Electricity is one of the most widely used forms of energy. It is a secondary energy source which is generated by the conversion of other sources of energy, like coal, natural gas, oil, nuclear power and other natural sources. These sources are called primary energy sources. Before electricity generation began over hundred years ago, houses were lit with kerosene lamps, food was cooled in iceboxes, and rooms were warmed by wood-burning or coal-burning stoves.

Benjamin Franklin is credited for the invention of electricity, due to the fact that idea of electricity began with Benjamin Franklin's experiment with a kite one stormy night in Philadelphia. In 1752, he proved that lightning and the spark from amber were the same thing. The story of this famous milestone is a familiar one, in which Franklin fastened an iron spike to a silken kite, which he flew during a thunderstorm, while holding the end of the kite string by an iron key. When lightning flashed, a tiny spark jumped from the key to his wrist. After this, the principles of electricity gradually became understood and electricity had been used in arc lights for outdoor lighting. In the mid of 19th century, everyone's life changed with the invention of the electric light bulb. This invention used electricity to bring indoor lighting to our homes.

ELECTRICITY

Basic properties of electric charges

Electric charge has three basic properties: quantisation, additivity and conservation.

Quantisation

Experimentally, it is established that all free charges are integral multiples of a basic unit of charge denoted by e. Thus, charge q on a body is always given by

q = ne

Where, n = 0, ±1, ±2, ±3, ...

The value of e is equal to -1.6 x 10^{-19} Coulomb. A proton and an electron have charges +e and –e respectively. For macroscopic charges, which have very large value of n, quantisation of charge can be ignored.

Additivity

Additivity of electric charges means that the total charge of a system is the algebraic sum of all individual charges in the system. If a system contains n point charges q^1, q^2, q^3······qn, then the total charge of the system will be $q^1 + q^2 + q^3 + \cdots + qn$.

Conservation: Charge, just like energy, can neither be created nor be destroyed. The total charge of an isolated system is always conserved i.e. it remains unchanged with time. Thus, when bodies are charged through friction, there is a transfer of electric charge from one body to another. There is no creation or destruction of charge.

Do it yourself

Attracting comb: Comb your hair vigorously and then bring the comb close to the paper.

Explanation: The electrons move to the comb due to rubbing, making it more negatively charged. So, it attracts positively charged objects such as a paper.

Conductors and insulators

The electrons of different types of atoms have different degrees of freedom to move around. The outermost electrons in the atoms of some materials are so loosely bound that they freely move in the space between the atoms of that material. They are called **free electrons**. Some materials have very little freedom for the electrons to move around. This relative mobility of electrons within a material is known as **electric conductivity**. Conductivity is determined by the types of atoms in a material and how the atoms are linked together with one another.

Conductors

Materials with high electron mobility are called conductors. They have many free electrons. They are called so because they conduct the electron current or flow of electrons easily.

For example: silver, copper, gold, aluminium, iron, steel, brass, bronze, mercury, graphite etc.

Insulators: Insulators are materials that have the opposite effect on the flow of electrons. They do not let electrons flow very easily from one atom to another. Their atoms have tightly bound electrons. Insulators are used to protect us from the dangerous effects of electricity flowing through conductors. The rubber coating on wires is an insulating material that shields us from the conductor wire inside.

For example: glass, rubber, oil, ceramic, quartz, plastic, diamond, pure water etc.

It must be understood that all conductive materials do not have the same level of conductivity. Similarly, not all insulators are equally resistant to electron motion. For example, the metals are good conductors of electricity, offering easier passage for electrons. Silver is considered as the best conductor. Dirty water is also a conductor but it is substantially less conductive than any metal.

Some materials experience changes in their electrical properties under different

ELECTRICITY

conditions. The good conductors can conduct electricity at room temperature.

Some materials, which have insulating properties at room temperature, can easily be influenced to be conductors by heating at high temperature. For example, glass is a very good insulator at room temperature. When we heat it at high temperature, temperature imparts conductivity to it and it acts as a conductor. Similarly, air is normally insulating but it becomes conductive if heated to very high temperatures.

The conductivity of most metals decreases with increasing temperature and increases with decreasing temperature. So, metals become better conductors when cooled. Many conductive materials become perfectly conductive when cooled at extremely low temperatures. This is called **superconductivity**.

Thomas Edison invented more than 2000 electric products, including switches, fuses, sockets and meters.

Methods of charging

There are three basic ways of charging an object. These are:

Charging by friction

If we rub two different materials together, they get charged by a process known as charging by friction. The frictional charging process is useful for charging insulators. This method results in a transfer of electrons between the two objects that are rubbed together. For example, rubber has a much greater attraction for electrons than animal fur. If they are rubbed together, the atoms of rubber pull electrons from the atoms of animal fur, leaving both objects with an imbalance of charge. The two objects become charged with opposite types of charges as a result of the transfer of electrons from the least electron-loving material to the most electron-loving material. Another good example is rubbing a glass rod with a piece of silk.

Charging by conduction

This method is useful for charging the

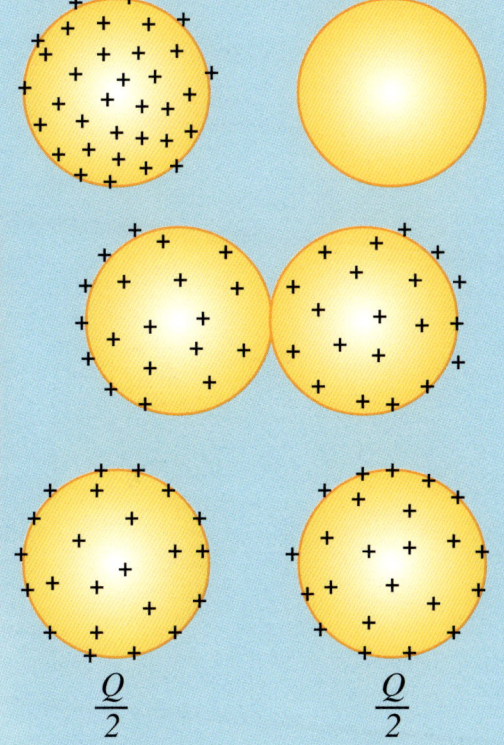

Do it yourself

Electricity can make heat: Feel an electric bulb which has not been used for a while. Then turn on the electricity and feel the bulb after one minute. The bulb gets warm.

Explanation: Part of the electrical energy is converted to heat as it passes through the wires (filament) in the bulb.

ELECTRICITY

conductors. Conduction means that the two objects will come into physical contact with each other. Thus, this method is generally known as 'charging by contact'.

If a charged object touches a conductor, some charge will be transferred between the object and the conductor, charging the conductor with the same sign as the charge on the object.

Charging by induction

Induction is the method to charge a conductor without coming into direct contact with it. Like conduction, a charged object is used in this method. But, the charged object is only brought close to the conductor and does not touch it. Charging by induction is a more complex process than conduction. The most important element is the use of a grounding wire. A grounding wire is simply a conductor that connects the object to the ground. The ground is basically anything neutral that can give up electrons to, or take electrons from, an object. If the conductor is connected to ground, electrons will either flow on to it or away from it. When the ground connection is snipped, the conductor will have a charge opposite in sign to that of the charged object.

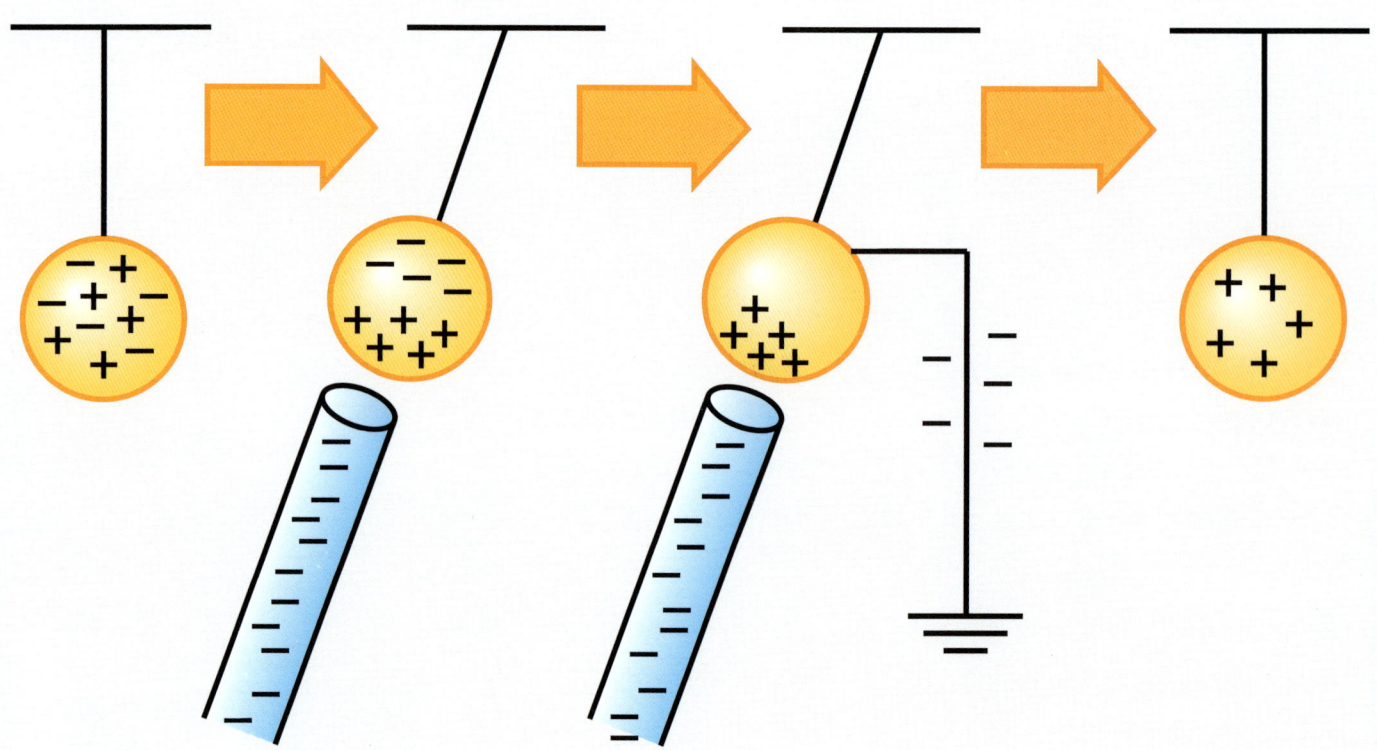

Force between electric charges

The force exerted by non-moving that is, static charges on each other is called the **electrostatic force**. The like charges always repel each other while opposite charges attract each other. Thus, the electrostatic force between the like charges is repulsive in nature while it is attractive between opposite charges.

Coulomb's law

French physicist Charles Augustine de Coulomb performed a series of experiments involving electric charges and eventually established the law of force between two electrostatic charges. This law is commonly known as Coulomb's

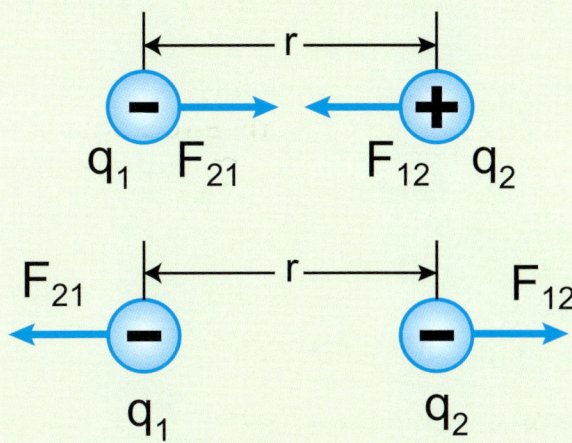

law. This law is a quantitative statement about the force between two point charges. When the linear size of charged bodies is much smaller than the distance separating them, their size maybe ignored. These charged bodies are termed as point charges.

The Coulomb's law states that 'the force between two point charges is inversely proportional to the square of the distance between the charges and directly proportional to the product of the magnitude of the two charges. This force acts along the line joining the two charges'.

Mathematically, if two point charges q_1 and q_2 are separated by a distance r, the magnitude of the force (F) between them is given by

$$F = k * q_1 q_2 / r^2$$

Where, k is a constant of proportionality which is equal to $8.99 \times 10^9 \, Nm^2/C^2$.

Electric field

An electric field is defined as the region surrounding a charged particle, Q, where another charged particle experiences either a force of attraction or repulsion. The electric field strength can be computed as

$E = k * Q / r^2$

The unit of electric field strength is Newton/Coulomb (N/C).

Electric field lines

Electric field lines are a way of pictorially mapping the electric field around a configuration of charges. These lines, in the form of the curves, are drawn in such a way that the tangent to them at each point is in the direction of the net field at the point. An arrow on them indicates the direction of the electric field. They point in the direction in which a positive charge responds to the electrostatic force. Thus, they are away from positive charges and towards negative charges.

Nature of the electric field lines

1. The electric lines of force of a positively charged body (i.e. q > 0) are directed away from the body.
2. The electric lines of force of a negatively charged body (i.e. q < 0) are directed towards the body.

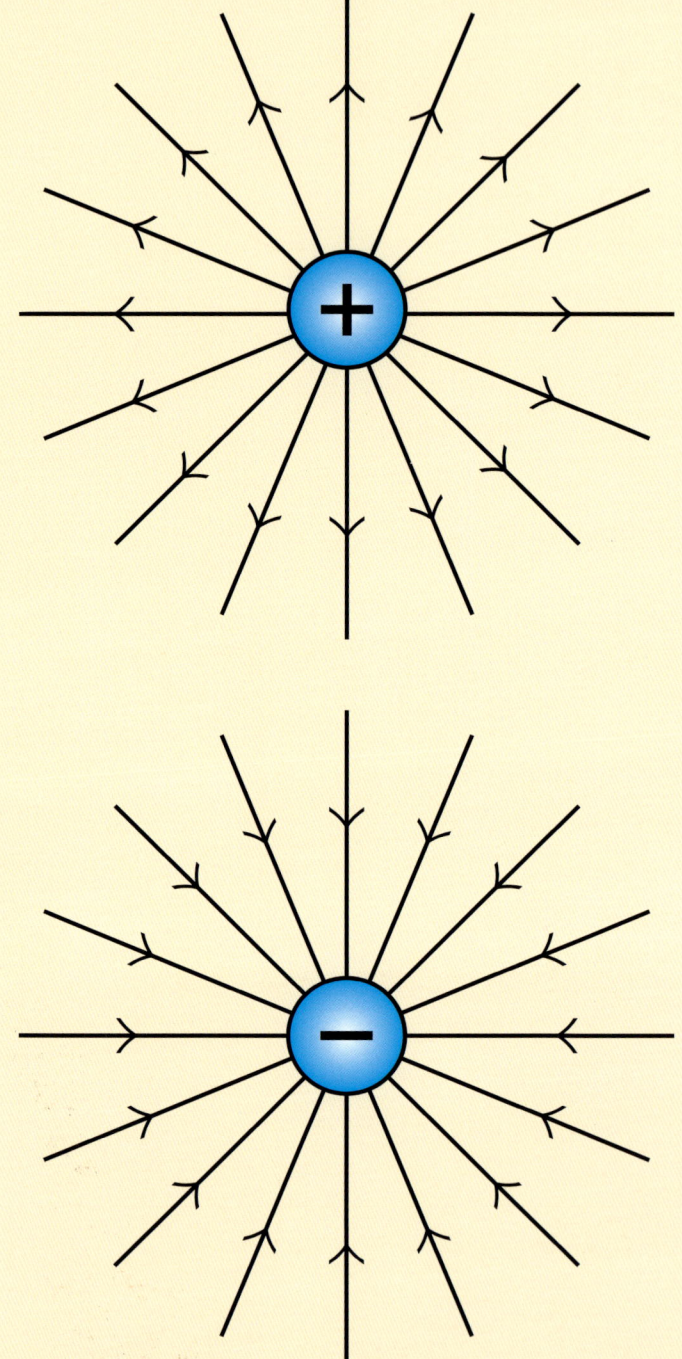

3. The electric lines of force give a dense picture of mutual repulsion when two positively charged bodies are put together in a system.
4. If two equal and opposite charges are

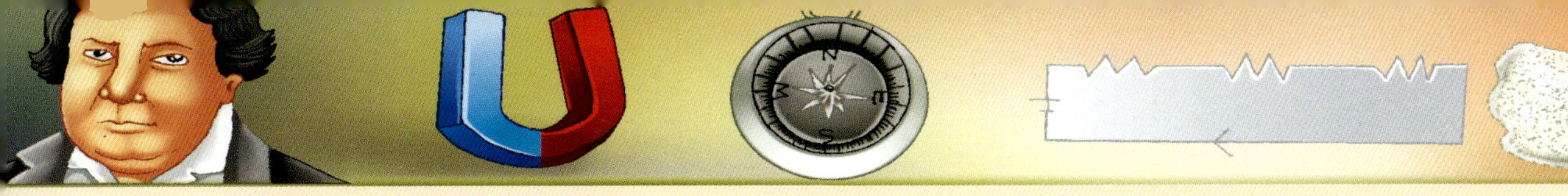

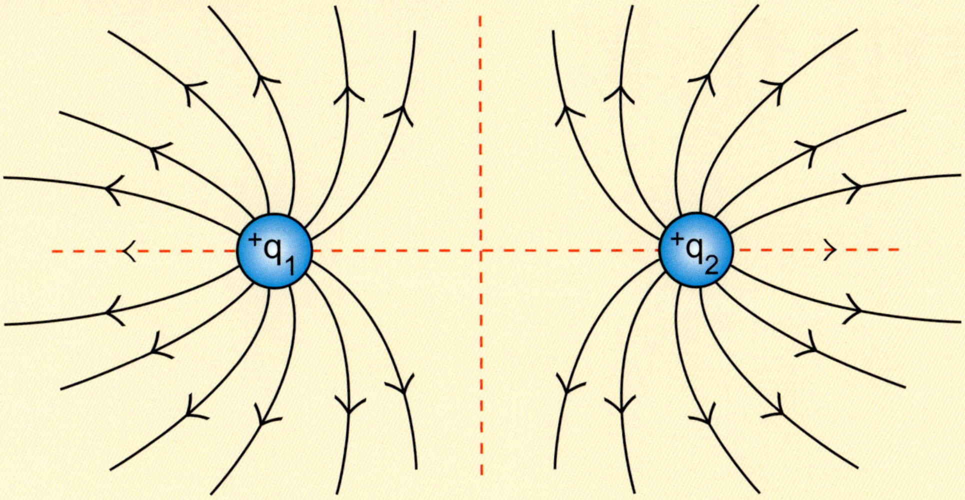

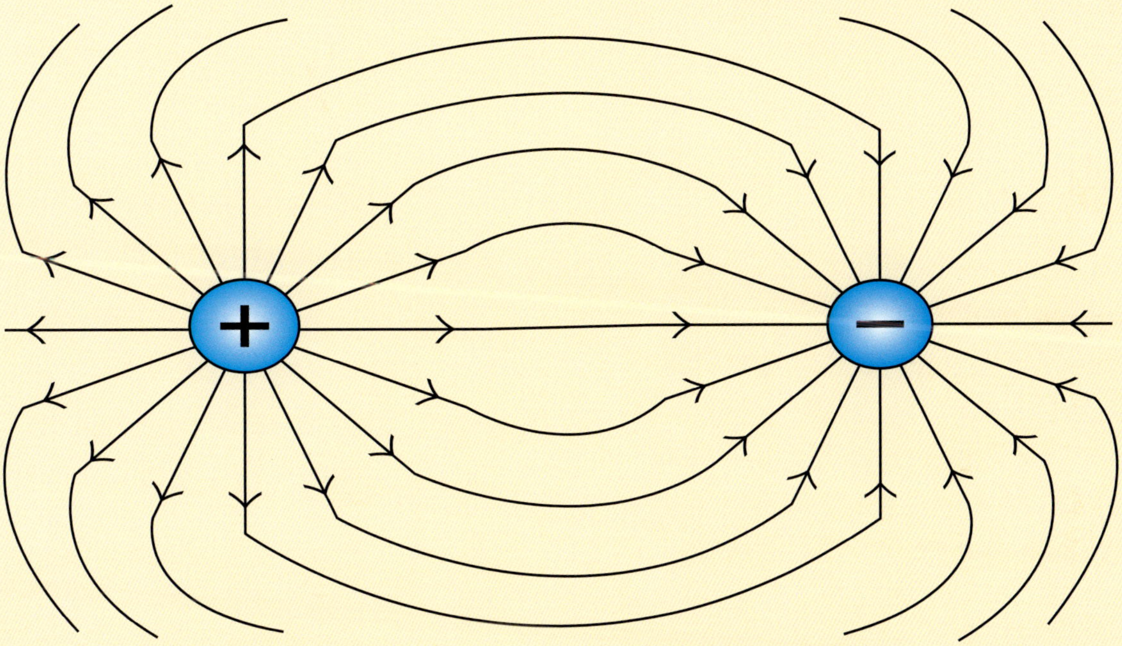

put together, the lines of force show mutual attraction. The lines move from positive charge to negative charge.

Properties of electric field lines

1. The lines of force start from positive charges and end at negative charges.
2. Two field lines can never intersect each other.
3. They exert lateral pressure on one another.
4. They are perpendicular to the surface of a charged conductor.
5. They do not pass through the conductor.

Electric flux

The number of field lines crossing a unit area is a measure of the strength of electric field. The strength of electric field at a point is known as **electric flux**. Thus, electric flux through an area is defined as the electric field multiplied by the area of the surface projected in a plane perpendicular to the field. It is represented by Φ. The flux of an electric field E at a small area element ΔS, is given by

$\Phi = E.\Delta S$

Gauss's Law

Gauss's law is a method to calculate the electric field of a given charge distribution. According to this law, the flux of electric field through any closed surface S is $1/\varepsilon_0$ times the total charge enclosed by S. The law is especially useful in determining electric field E, when the source distribution has simple symmetry. Mathematically, we can say

$\Phi = E.\Delta S$

On putting, $\Delta S = 1/\varepsilon_0$

$\Phi = Q.\, 1/\varepsilon_0$

If $Q = 0$, Φ also becomes zero.

Thus, this law implies that the total electric flux through a closed surface is zero if no charge is enclosed by the surface.

> One modern power plant can produce enough electricity for 1,80,000 houses. The first power plant was owned by Thomas Edison and it was opened in New York in 1882.

Do it yourself

Electromagnets: You can easily build your own electromagnet at home. Get about five metres of copper magnet wire, a large iron nail, a rubber band, some sandpapers and a small battery. Wind all of the wire around the iron nail. Using the sandpaper, remove the enamel coating from the each end of copper wire. Now connect these ends to the battery, one wire touching the negative end and one wire touching the positive end. Use the rubber band to hold the wires in place. Use it to attract paper clips. Does it?

Electric potential

Electric potential is defined as the amount of work done to move a unit charge from one point to another point against an electric field. Let us consider a positive charge 'q' located between two plates, A and B, of an electric field 'E'. The electric force 'F' exerted by the field on the positive charge can be given as

F = qE

To move the charge from plate A to plate B, we must apply an equal and opposite force (i.e. F' = -qE). The work done in moving the positive charge through a distance 'd' can be calculated as

Work done = F' * d
          = -qE * d

This is also known as the electric potential energy of a charge. If an electric field is defined as the force per unit charge, then an electric potential can be defined as the potential energy per unit charge. Therefore, the work done in moving a unit charge from one point to another is equal to the difference in potential energies at each point. This is also commonly known as electric potential difference and is represented by symbol 'V'. The potential energy of a positive charge increases when it moves against an electric field and decreases when it moves with the electric field. The opposite is true for negative charges.

In the International System of Units (SI), the unit of electric potential is joules per coulomb (J/C). It is commonly known as volt.

Equipotential lines trace lines of equal electric potential. These are always perpendicular to the electric field.

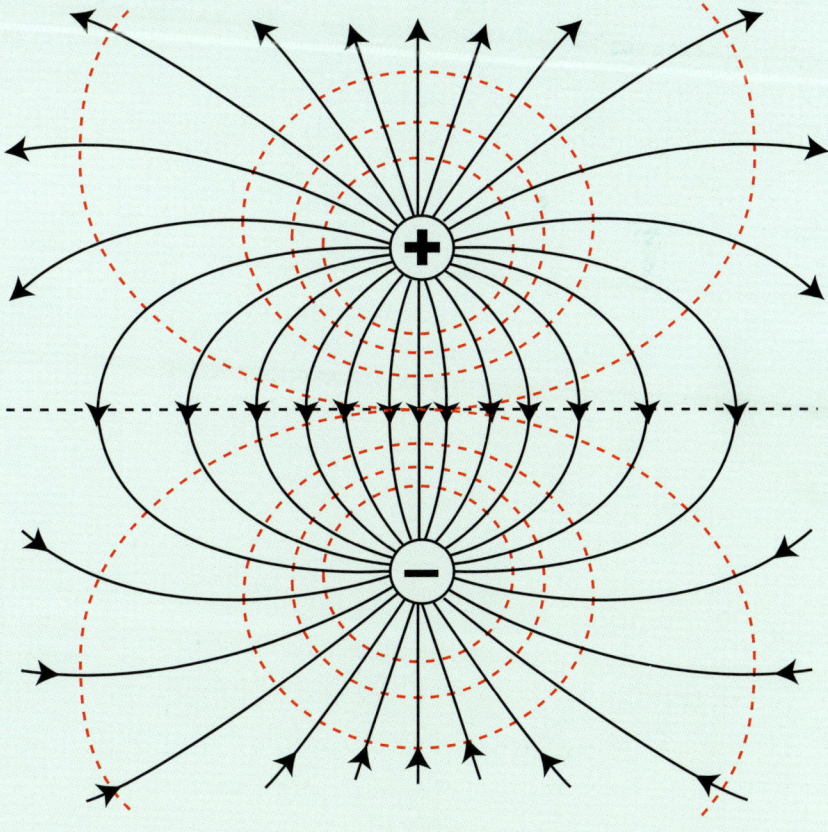

Equipotential lines

Capacitors and capacitance

A capacitor is a system of two conductors separated by an insulator.

Consider two conductors having charges Q_1 and Q_2 and electric potential of V_1 and V_2. Then, in configuration of a capacitor, Q and $-Q$ is the magnitude of charges on the two conductors and V is the potential difference between them.

The electric field in the region between the conductors follows from the direct proportionality between field and charge implied by Coulomb's law. The electric field is directly proportional to the charge Q. That is, if the charge on the capacitor is, say doubled, the electric field will also be doubled at every point. The potential difference V is also proportional to Q and the ratio Q/V is a constant.

$$Q / V = C$$

Where, C is determined purely geometrically, by the shapes, sizes and relative positions of the two conductors. The constant C is called the **capacitance** of the capacitor. For a parallel plate capacitor (where two plate conductors each with area A are separated by distance d with vacuum between the plates),

$$C = \varepsilon_0 A / d$$

The conductors may be so charged by connecting them to the two terminals of a battery. The total charge of the capacitor is zero. The unit of capacitance is farad. By definition, one farad is equal to one coulomb per volt.

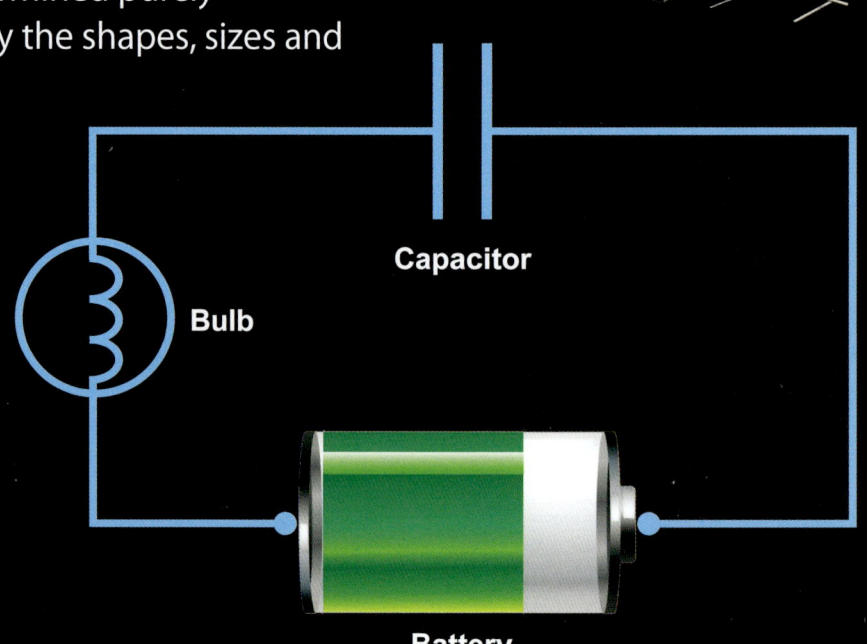

Combinations of capacitors

The capacitors are combined to obtain greater capacitance for different purposes. The capacitors can be combined in parallel or series.

Capacitors in series

Suppose, we have n number capacitors with capacitance $C_1, C_2, C_3, ..., C_n$ and combine them in series. Then, the total capacitance C is given by

$$1/C = 1/C_1 + 1/C_2 + 1/C_3 + \cdots\cdots + C_n$$

Capacitors in parallel

Suppose, we have n number capacitors with capacitance $C_1, C_2, C_3, ..., C_n$ and combine them in parallel. Then, the total capacitance C is given by

$$C = C_1 + C_2 + C_3 + ...$$

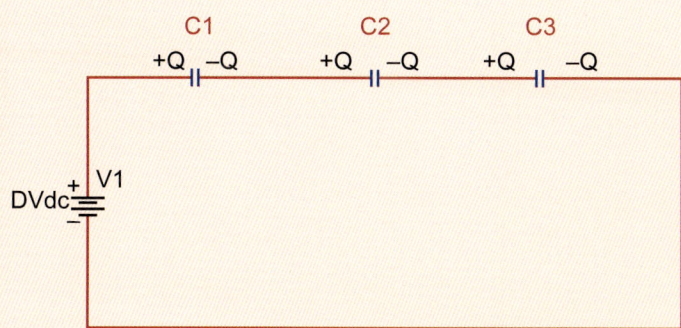
Capacitors in series combination

Energy storage in a capacitor

The total energy (E) stored in a capacitor of capacitance C, with charge Q and voltage V can be calculated as

$$E = ½ QV$$
$$= ½ CV^2$$
$$= ½ Q^2/C$$

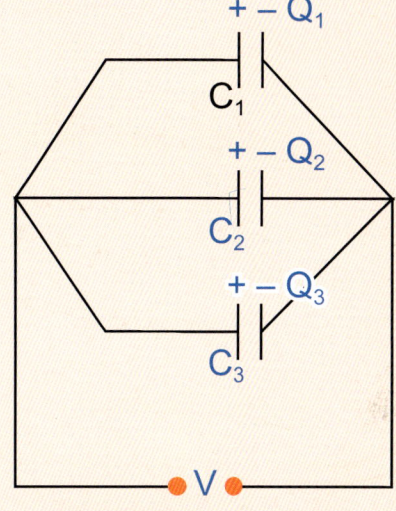
Capacitors in parallel combination

You may have heard of direct current (DC) and alternating current (AC). The difference between the two is in the way the electrons flow. In DC electrons move in a single direction while in AC they change directions, switching between backwards and forwards. The electricity use in your home is AC while DC comes from sources that include batteries. Back in the 1880's there was even a 'war of currents' between Thomas Edison (who invented DC) and Nikola Tesla (who invented AC). Both wanted their system to be used. AC eventually won due to the fact that it is safer and can be used over longer distances.

ELECTRICITY

Electric current

Current is defined as the rate at which charges move forward in a circuit. Let us suppose Q be the net charge flowing across a cross section of a conductor. Then, the current at time t across the cross-section of the conductor is defined as the ratio of charge and time. The current is represented by symbol I and expressed as

$I = Q / t$

The unit of current is ampere (A). By definition, one ampere is equal to one coulomb of charge moving through a capacitor in one second. An ampere is typically the order of magnitude of currents in most of the domestic appliances. Small appliances may have microamperes. Also, the currents in our nerves are of order of microamperes. A lightning may carry high currents of the order of tens of thousands of amperes.

Current density is defined as the current per unit area taken normal to the current and is denoted by j. Thus,

$J = I / A$

The SI unit of the current density is A/m2.

Also, if E is the magnitude of uniform electric field in the conductor whose length is ℓ, then the potential difference V across its ends is given as

$V = E \ell$

Electricity plays an important role in the way our heart beats. Muscle cells in the heart are contracted by electricity going through the heart. Electrocardiogram (ECG) machines used in hospitals measure the electricity going through a person's heart. When the person is healthy, it usually shows a line moving across a screen with regular spikes as the heart beats.

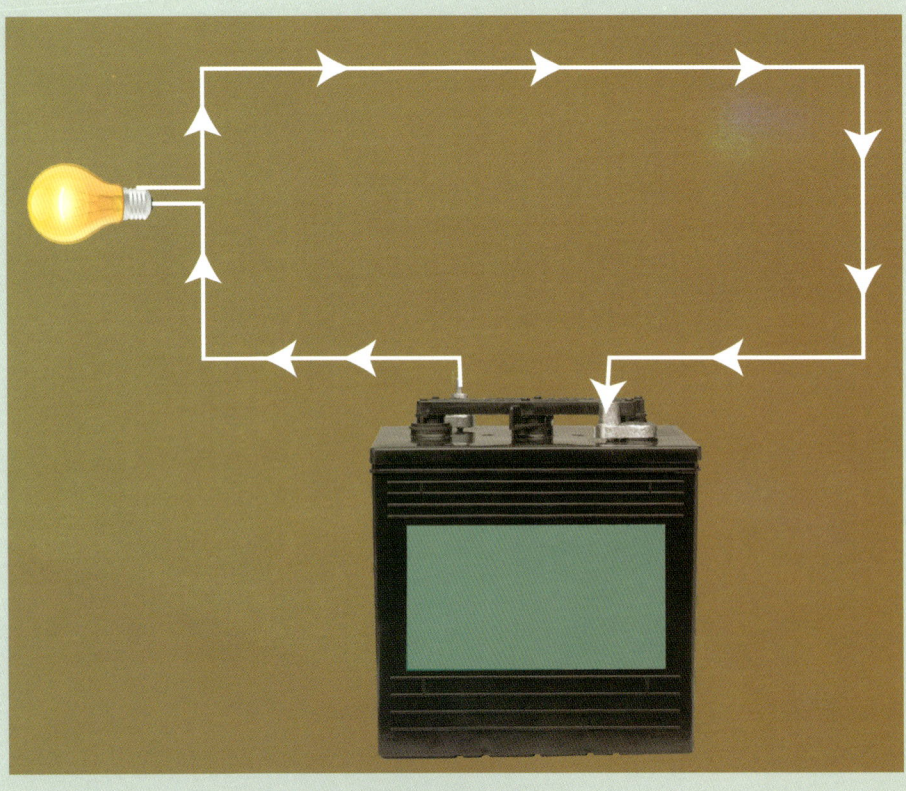
Electric Current

Ohm's law

Ohm's law is the basic law regarding flow of currents. It was formulated by G.S. Ohm in 1828. Imagine a conductor through which a current (I) is flowing and V is the potential difference between the ends of the conductor. Then, Ohm's law states that

$V \propto I$

$V = R I$

Where, R is the constant of proportionality known as the resistance of the conductor. The SI unit of resistance is ohm and we denote it by the symbol Ω. One ohm is the resistance value through which one volt will maintain a current of one ampere.

The resistance depends on the material of the conductor as well as on the dimensions of the conductor. It is directly proportional to length and inversely proportional to area of the conductor. Thus,

$R \propto \ell / A$

Where, ℓ is the length and A is the area of the conductor.

$R = \rho \ell / A$

ρ is the constant of proportionality which only depends on the material of the conductor and is called *resistivity*.

Thus, we can rewrite equation V=IR as,

$V = I \rho \ell / A$

What all are attracted to magnets?

Take a strong magnet and go around the house to see what will stick to it. Keep a list of the items you tried and select those which were attracted to magnet. Also, observe if the attraction was strong, weak, or none.

Try especially different types of metals, for example: iron (nails, screws and nuts), stainless steel (everyday forks and spoons, brass (kick-plates on front doors), zinc (battery case), copper (old pennies, copper wires), bronze (marine bell), aluminium (kitchen foils), silver (jewellery), gold (wedding rings or other jewellery).

Resistance

Resistance determines the amount of current flow through a component. Resistors are generally used to control voltage and current levels. The flow of current is inversely related to the resistance. According to ohm's law, we know that

$V = IR$

$I = V/R$

$I \propto 1/R$

Thus, high resistance allows a small amount of current to flow while low resistance allows a large amount of current to flow. Now it is clear to us that resistance slows down the flow of charge in a circuit. We know that resistance is represented by symbol R and it is measured in units called Ohms with the symbol (Ω).

1 Ohm = 1 Volt / 1 Ampere

All conductors have some resistance. Commercially produced resistors are of two major types— wire bound resistors and carbon resistors. Wire bound resistors are made by winding the wires. The choice of the wire materials depends on the fact that their resistivity is insensitive to the temperature. These resistances are in the range of a fraction of an ohm to a few hundred ohms. Carbon resistors are made to provide high resistance. Carbon resistors are compact and inexpensive. They are extensively used in electronic circuits.

1. We know that the resistance depends on the material of the conductor as well as on the dimensions of the conductor and given as

   $R = \rho \ell / A$

Where, ρ is the constant of proportionality which only depends on the material of

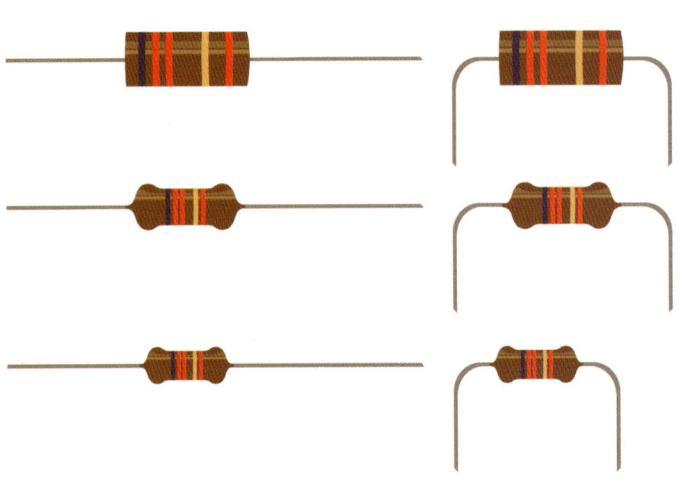

Resistors

Resistance

the conductor and is called *resistivity*. Resistivity of different substances varies over a very wide range. Metals have very low resistivity, that's why they are good conductors. Insulators like glass and rubber have higher resistivity. Thus, they are bad conductors and resist the flow of electricity.

Combination of resistors

Resistors in series: The resistors are said to be in series if only one of their end points is joined. If we connect *n* resistors in series, the total resistance R is given as

$R = R_1 + R_2 + ... + R_n$

Resistors in parallel: The resistors are said to be connected in parallel if one end of all the resistors is joined together and similarly the other ends also joined together. If we connect n resistors in parallel, the total resistance R is given as

$1/R = 1/R_1 + 1/R_2 + 1/R_3 + \cdots\cdots + 1/R_n$

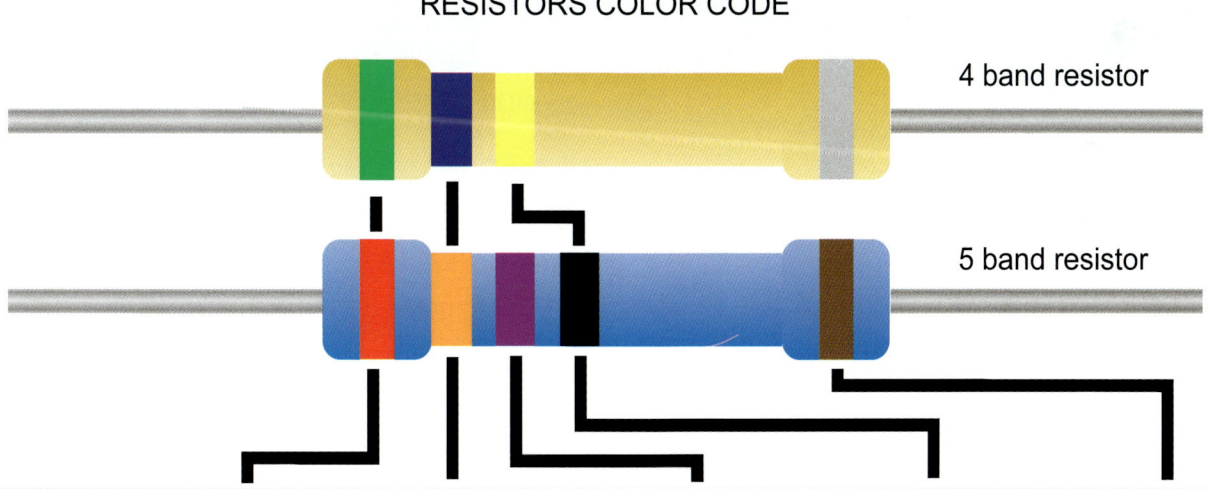

RESISTORS COLOR CODE

Color	1st Band	2nd Band	3rd Band	Multiplier	Tolerance
Black	0	0	0	× 1 Ω	
Brown	1	1	1	× 10 Ω	+/− 1%
Red	2	2	2	× 100 Ω	+/− 2%
Orange	3	3	3	× 1K Ω	
Yellow	4	4	4	× 10K Ω	
Green	5	5	5	× 100K Ω	+/− 5%
Blue	6	6	6	× 1M Ω	+/− 25%
Violet	7	7	7	× 10M Ω	+/− .1%
Grey	8	8	8		+/− .05%
White	9	9	9		
Gold				× .1 Ω	+/− 5%
Silver				× .01 Ω	+/− 10%

Resistors in series

We can easily understand the theory of combinations of resistors in electric circuits using Ohm's law. Suppose two resistors R_1 and R_2 are connected in series. By rule, the charge which leaves R_1 must be entering R_2. Since current is defined as the rate of flow of charge, the same current I will flow through R_1 and R_2.

If we apply Ohm's law:

Potential difference across R_1, $V_1 = I R_1$

Potential difference across R_2, $V_2 = I R_2$

The potential difference V across the combination will be $V_1 + V_2$.

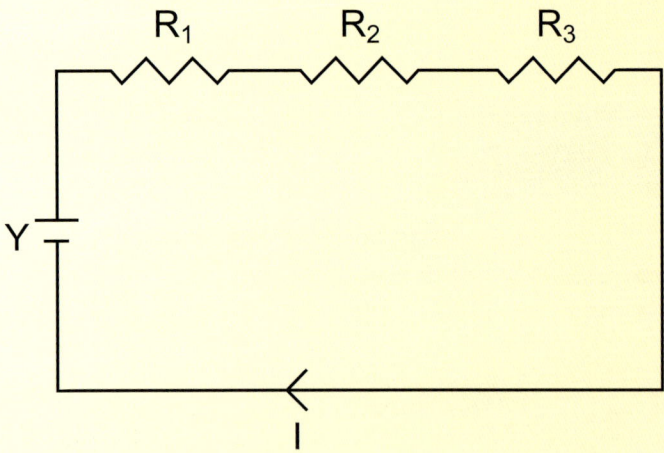

Thus,

$V = V_1 + V_2$
$ = I(R_1 + R_2)$

The total resistance of combination can be calculated by Ohm's law as

$V = I R$

$R = V / I$

$R = I(R_1 + R_2) / I = (R_1 + R_2)$

Similarly, it can be extended to a series combination of n number of resistors R_1, R_2 ....., R_n. The resistance of combination will be

$R = R_1 + R_2 + ... + R_n$

Make your own potato battery

Arrange potato, 2 pennies, 2 galvanized nails, three 8 inch lengths insulated copper wire, each with 2 inches of the insulation stripped off one end and a digital clock with attachments for wires. First, cut a potato in half and put the two halves on a plate so they stand on their flat ends. Wrap the end of one piece of wire around a galvanized nail and wrap the end of a second piece of wire around a penny. Stick the nail and penny into one half of the potato so that they're not touching each other. Now, wrap the third piece of wire around the other penny and put it into the other half of the potato. Put the other nail into the second half of the potato, but this nail should not have wire wrapped around it. Now, connect the wire from the penny on the first half of the potato to the nail that has no wire on it in the second half of the potato. Finally, touch the free ends of the wires to the wires coming out of the digital clock. Does it work?

Resistors in parallel

Now let us learn how we can apply Ohm's law for understanding combination of resistors in parallel. Suppose two resistors R_1 and R_2 are connected in parallel. By definition, the charge that enters to circuit will flow out partly through R_1 and partly through R_2. Let us consider that current I_1 and I_2 will flow through R_1 and R_2 respectively. The total current that flows through circuit will be

$$I = I_1 + I_2$$

If we apply Ohm's law:

Potential difference across R_1, $\quad V = I_1 R_1$

$$I_1 = V / R_1$$

Potential difference across R_2, $\quad V = I_2 R_2$

$$I_2 = V / R_2$$

Since, $\quad I = I_1 + I_2$

$$= V / R_1 + V / R_2$$
$$= V (1/R_1 + 1/R_2)$$

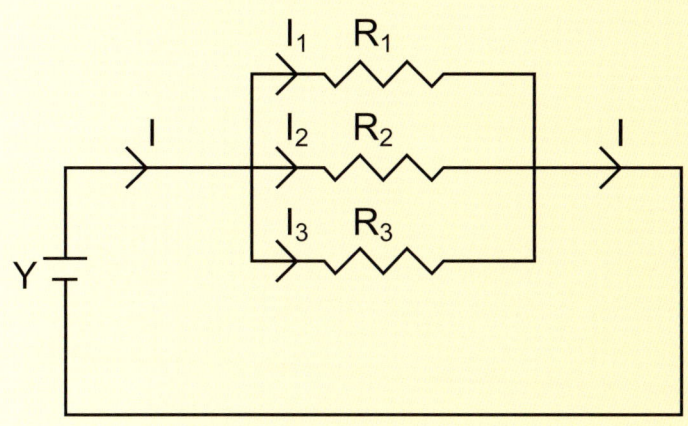

If resistance of combination is R, then by Ohm's law

$$V = I R$$
$$I = V / R$$

Comparing this equation with above equation, we get

$$1/R = 1/R_1 + 1/R_2$$

Similarly, it can be extended to a parallel combination of n number of resistors R_1, R_2 ....., R_n. The resistance of combination will be

$$1/R = 1/R_1 + 1/R_2 + 1/R_3 + \cdots + 1/R_n$$

How to make a magnetic compass?

Arrange one needle and a strong magnet. Lay just the eye of the needle over any magnet and leave it there overnight, after which the needle will have become a magnet. The next day, stick the needle through a small piece of cork. Take a bowl of water and fill it about halfway. Now, drop the cork with the needle in the middle of the bowl. What do you see? You can see that the needle slowly turns until it is pointing in a certain direction. Finally, give the needle a little spin and observe where it settles.

Is it pointing towards north or south? If yes, then congratulations, you've made your first compass.

Electric power

Let us consider a conductor with end points A and B, in which a current I is flowing from A to B. The electric potential at A and B are denoted by V_1 and V_2 respectively. As current is flowing from A to B, by definition

$V_1 > V_2$

If electric potential difference across AB is V, then

$V = V_1 - V_2$

We know that the charge between two points in time t is given by

$Q = I * t$

By definition, the potential energy of the charge at A will be $Q*V_1$ and similarly at B, it is QV_2. The change in potential energy (ΔU) can be denoted as

ΔU = Final potential energy – Initial potential energy

$= QV_2 - QV_1 = Q[V_2 - V_1]$

$= -QV$

$= -IV*t$

The energy dissipated per unit time is known as the **electric power**. It is represented by P and can be given as

$P = \Delta U/t$

On putting the value of ΔU, from above equation;

$P = IV$

We know that according to Ohm's law V = IR, we get

$P = I^2 R = V^2/R$

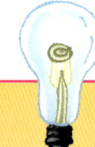

Do it yourself

The poles of a magnet have maximum strength

Lower a magnet of any type into a pile of nails or clips or pins. Try picking up the nails with the different parts of the magnet. What do you observe?

Explanation: The nails cling to the ends of the magnet. So, a magnet has the strongest attraction at its ends. These are known as the north and south poles of the magnet.

Magnetism

Magnetism is defined as the force exerted by a magnetic object through its magnetic field, on another object in its magnetic field. The two objects do not essentially need to be physically attached for the force to be exerted. Objects feel the magnetic force due to the surrounding magnetic field.

Magnetic field

A magnetic field is a region in space where a magnet or a ferromagnetic object experiences a non-contact force. In most materials these fields point in all directions, so the net magnetic field is zero. In ferromagnetic materials, there are regions called **domains**, where magnetic fields line up. All the atoms in each domain group together so that the magnetic fields from

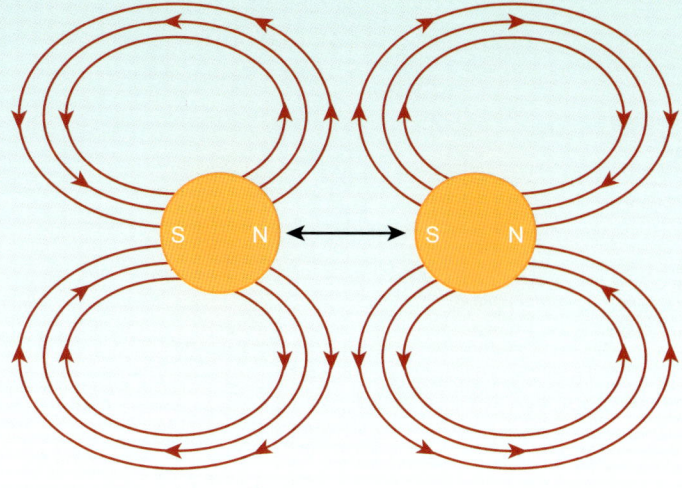

their electrons point in the same direction. The magnets have a pair of opposite poles, called north (N) and south (S). If we cut the magnet into tiny pieces, each piece will have both of the poles N and S. These poles always occur in pairs. In nature, we can never find a north magnetic pole or south magnetic pole on its own.

Like poles of magnets always repel each other while unlike poles attract. So, two N poles or two S poles push away from each other while N pole and S pole attract each other.

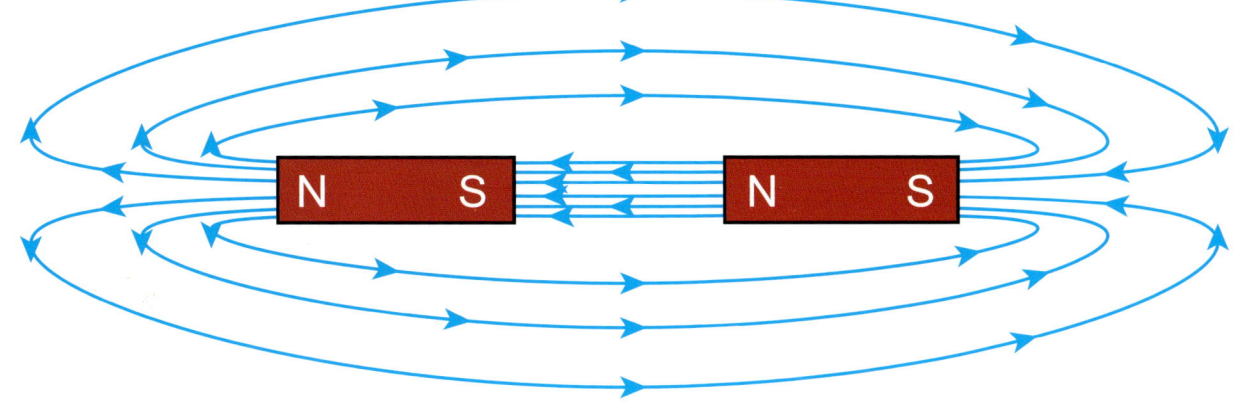

Magnetic field lines

Magnetic fields are represented using magnetic field lines. In domains where the magnetic field is strong, the field lines are closer together. The strength of a magnetic field is known as the **magnetic flux**.

Characteristics of magnetic field lines

1. They never cross each other.
2. Arrows on the field lines indicate the direction of the field.
3. A magnetic field points from the north to the south pole of a magnet.

Magnetic compass

A compass is a magnetic instrument used to find the direction of a magnetic field. A

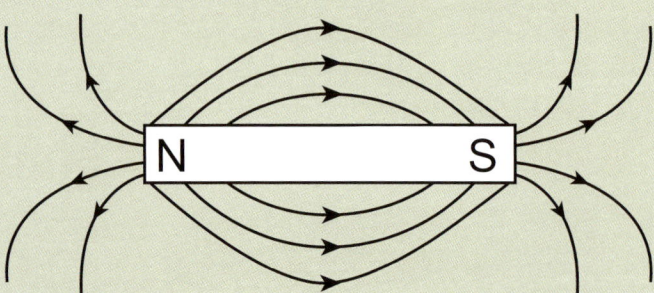

compass consists of a small metal needle which is magnetised and free to turn in any direction. So, in the presence of a magnetic field, the needle lines up in the direction of the magnetic field. Compasses are commonly used in navigation to find directions on the earth. The common compass works by Earth's magnetic field. The compass needle aligns itself with the magnetic field direction and points towards north or south.

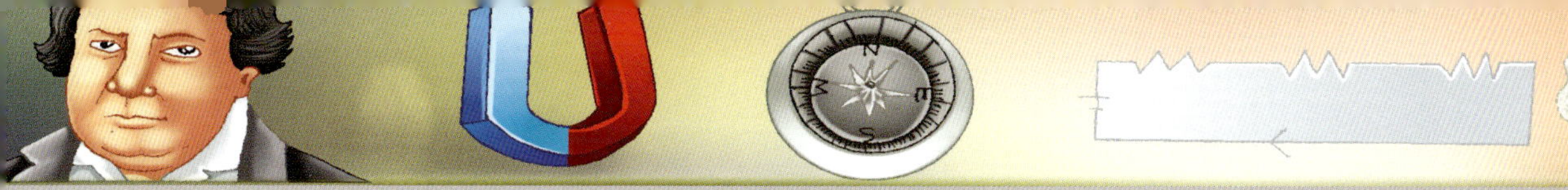

Voltmeter

A voltmeter is a device to measure the voltage passing between two points of a circuit. A Voltmeter can be called a versatile instrument because it measures not only voltage but also current and resistance. The voltmeter measures voltage by passing current through a resistance. It is designed in such a way that it offers minimum disturbance to the circuit. This is achieved by using a sensitive ammeter in series with a high resistance. The sensitivity of a voltmeter is depicted in ohms/ volt.

There are several types of voltmeters in use today, the most common being digital voltmeters that use the natural resistance of electric circuits. Voltmeter is one of the most commonly used testing equipment that measures differences of electrical potential between two points in an electric circuit. Now a day, the multipurpose voltmeters generally come combined with ammeter and ohmmeter.

Uses of a voltmeter

1. Voltage measurement
2. Electrical testing
3. Educational laboratory
4. Electronics industry

Ammeter

Ammeter is an instrument that measures either direct or alternating electric current, in amperes. A simple ammeter can measure a wide range of current values. At higher currents, only a small portion of the current is directed through the meter mechanism, while a shunt in parallel with the meter carries the major portion.

In other words, an ammeter is an electronic measuring instrument that evaluates the flow of electric current in an electronic circuit. An ammeter measures the flow of current in amperes (A). The various ammeters available in the market are able to measure the amount and rate of current in both small and large electrical devices. The device is handy for measuring the flow of current through the wiring systems of society buildings, ensuring the wiring is up to acceptable local safety codes. Companies that manufacture electrical equipment use an ammeter for testing the products before offering them for sale.

A very simple ammeter employs the process of magnetic deflection in order to measure the flow of amperes through a given circuit. It is constructed with a moving coil design in such a way that the device could be attached to a circuit. With the flow of current into the device, the coil begins to shift within the magnetic field. The degree of shift and movement of the coil determine the flow of the current.

The Ancient Greek philosopher Thales noticed that amber decorations on spinning wheels attracted threads, feathers, and other objects through what we now know to be static electricity. The Greek word for amber is elektron, from which William Gilbert, physician to Queen Elizabeth I, coined the word "electricity".

Wattmeter

A wattmeter is an instrument which is used to measure electric power. This instrument consists of a pair of fixed coils, known as current coils, and a movable coil known as the potential coil. The fixed coils are made up of a few turns of a large conductor. The potential coil consists of many turns of fine wires. It is mounted on a shaft, carried in bearings, so that it may turn inside the stationary coils. The movable potential coil carries a needle which moves over a suitably marked scale. Spiral coil springs hold this needle to a start zero position.

The stationary current coil of the wattmeter is connected in series with the circuit, and the movable potential coil is connected across the line. When current flows through the current coil of a wattmeter, a field sets up around the coil. The strength of electric field is directly proportional to the line current. The potential coil of the wattmeter generally has a high-resistance resistor which is connected in series with it. The main purpose is to make the potential-coil circuit of the meter as resistive as possible. As a result, current in the potential circuit is in phase with line voltage. And, when voltage is applied to the potential circuit, current is proportional to and in phase with the line voltage. The force of a wattmeter comes from the field of its current coil and the field of its potential coil. The force acting on the movable coil at any instant is proportional to the instantaneous values of line current and voltage.

> **Electricity travels at the speed of light. It can be made from wind, water, sunlight and even from animal manure.**

Tips to save electricity

- ✓ Use heaters to heat only the rooms you're in rather than a central system that heats the whole house and turn off the heater when you're not home.

- ✓ Replace more energy consuming old appliances with energy saving star rated appliances.

- ✓ Use ceiling fans instead of air conditioners.

- ✓ Turn off all the lights you're not using.

- ✓ Dry your clothes on a laundry rack instead of using a dryer.

- ✓ Turn off computers, monitors, power strips, printers and copiers when you are not using.

- ✓ Wash laundry in cold water instead of hot water.

- ✓ Replace 100-watt or 60-watt light bulbs with compact fluorescent lights (CFLs).

- ✓ It is better to use staircase whenever possible than elevators because it saves electricity as well as makes our body healthier.

- ✓ Turning off is not enough as it leaves the idle power on still sucking electricity. To stop the flow, we must unplug the unit. It could save 10-15 per cent of our electricity.

Test Your MEMORY

1. What are charged particles?

2. Differentiate between conductors and insulators?

3. Explain Coulomb's law?

4. Define electric potential?

5. Describe Ohm's law?

6. What are the different methods of charging?

7. Write the properties of electric lines?

8. Define a capacitor and capacitance?

9. What do you understand by electric current?

10. Define resistance?

11. Give an account of magnetism.

12. What do voltmeter, ammeter and wattmeter measure?

ELECTRICITY

Index

A
additivity 6
aluminium 19
ammeter 27, 28
attraction 9, 12, 13, 19, 24

B
brass 7, 19
bronze 7, 19

C
capacitance 16, 17
capacitor 16, 17, 18
capacitors in parallel 17
capacitors in series 17
ceramic 7
charging by conduction 9
charging by friction 9
charging by induction 10
conductivity 7, 8
conductors 7, 8, 10, 16, 20, 21
constant of proportionality 11, 19, 20
copper 7, 14, 19, 22
coulomb 4, 6, 15, 16, 18
Coulomb's law 11, 16
current 7, 18, 19, 20, 22, 23, 24, 27, 28, 29
current coils 29
current density 18

D
degrees of freedom 7
diamond 7
digital voltmeters 27

E
electric charges 3, 6, 11
electric field 12, 13, 14, 15, 16, 18, 29
electric field lines 12, 13
electric flux 14
electric potential 15, 16, 24
electric potential energy 15
electric power 24, 29
electron 4, 6, 7, 9
electrostatic force 11, 12

F
free electrons 7

G
Gauss's law 14
glass 7, 8, 9, 21
gold 7, 19
graphite 7

I
insulators 7, 9, 21
iron 5, 7, 14, 19

M
magnetic compass 23, 26
magnetic field 25, 26, 28
magnetic field lines 26
magnetism 25
mercury 7
microCoulombs 4

N
nanoCoulombs 4
neutral objects 3

O
ohm 19, 20
Ohm's law 19, 20, 22, 23, 24
oil 5, 7

P
plastic 7
point charges 6, 11
potential coil 29
proton 4, 6

Q
quartz 7

R
repulsion 12
resistance 19, 20, 21, 22, 23, 27, 29
resistivity 19, 20, 21
resistors in parallel 21, 23
resistors in series 21, 22
rubber 7, 9, 14, 21

S
shunt 28
silver 7, 19
steel 7
superconductivity 8

V
volt 15, 16, 19, 27
voltmeter 27

W
wattmeter 29